W9-CGU-234

55
FAMOUS QUILTS
FROM
THE SHELBURNE MUSEUM
IN FULL COLOR

EDITED BY

CELIA Y. OLIVER
Curator, Shelburne Museum

PUBLISHED IN ASSOCIATION WITH THE
SHELBURNE MUSEUM
BY
DOVER PUBLICATIONS, INC.
NEW YORK

FRONTISPIECE:

Sawtooth Diamond in Square Quilt, pieced and quilted, maker unknown, Lancaster County, Pennsylvania, cotton and wool, c. 1900 (83″ × 82″)
GIFT OF JAMES WATSON WEBB, JR.

The Amish are known for their strict piety, separation from the secular world and self-sustaining community life centered on farm, family and church. The simple geometric forms used in their quilt patterns are dramatically different from the ornate pieced, appliqué and embroidered quilts popular in late Victorian America. The Center Diamond or Diamond in Square, made almost exclusively by Lancaster County Amish, is one of the oldest and plainest patterns used. The severity of the pattern is relieved by the sawtooth edging just as the pattern areas are relieved with elaborate quilting.

Copyright © 1990 by the Shelburne Museum.
All rights reserved under Pan American and International Copyright Conventions.

Published in Canada by General Publishing Company, Ltd., 30 Lesmill Road, Don Mills, Toronto, Ontario.
Published in the United Kingdom by Constable and Company, Ltd., 3 The Lanchesters, 162–164 Fulham Palace Road, London W6 9ER.

55 Famous Quilts from the Shelburne Museum in Full Color is a new work, first published by Dover Publications, Inc., in 1990 in association with the Shelburne Museum, Shelburne, Vermont.

Manufactured in the United States of America
Dover Publications, Inc., 31 East 2nd Street, Mineola, N.Y. 11501

Library of Congress Cataloging-in-Publication Data

Shelburne Museum.
    55 famous quilts from the Shelburne Museum in full color / edited by Celia Y. Oliver.
        p.   cm. — (Dover needlework series)
    Includes index.
    ISBN 0-486-26474-2 (pbk)
    1. Quilts—United States—Catalogs. 2. Quilts—Vermont—Shelburne—Catalogs. 3. Shelburne Museum—Catalogs. I. Oliver, Celia Y. II. Title. III. Title: Fifty-five famous quilts from the Shelburne Museum in full color. IV. Series.
NK9112.S46   1990
746.9′7′09740747474317—dc20   90-43789
                                                                                    CIP

INTRODUCTION

The Shelburne Museum was founded in 1947 by Electra Havemeyer Webb (1888–1960), an early and pioneering collector of Americana, as a home for her unique and eclectic collections. The Museum's collections directly reflect Mrs. Webb's passionate interest in American decorative, folk and fine arts. From the first, she envisioned a museum that would deepen visitors' appreciation for the beauty and ingenuity that our predecessors incorporated into the tools, toys and furnishings of their everyday lives.

ELECTRA HAVEMEYER WEBB, C. 1954

Electra Havemeyer Webb was the daughter of Horace O. and Louisine Havemeyer. They were noted col-lectors of European art who, with the help of Mary Cassatt, were among the first Americans to seriously acquire works by contemporary French artists. Living with avid collectors and surrounded by masterpieces in her home, Electra developed a strong interest in art and in forming a collection of her own. During a trip to Europe she described her feelings in a letter to her future husband, James Watson Webb: "I would like to be so rich that I could buy any works of Art I wanted. . . . How anyone can like Jewels when they can buy pictures." In another letter she described a recent purchase, "I spent a very large sum for a picture by Goya. . . . It is a portrait of a small girl of six, too cunning and sweet but really very fine. I am so pleased to feel that I am starting a collection as that is certainly what I intend doing with father's money."

After their marriage in 1910, James Watson and Electra Webb often visited the Webb family estate in Shelburne, Vermont. Enjoying their visits to the country, but wanting a home of their own, they requested the use of a small brick farmhouse at the southern end of the estate. When faced with decorating "the Brick House," Electra searched for an alternative to the ornate decorating style favored by her mother and mother-in-law. In keeping with the informal and relaxed lifestyle she and her husband enjoyed in Vermont, Mrs. Webb began to acquire and fill the house with locally procured country-style furniture and acces-sories, what her appalled mother called "kitchen furni-ture." As her interest in Americana grew, so did the accumulation of furnishings and art work indigenous to New England. "The Brick House" filled with Windsor chairs, country tables and cupboards, hand-painted and early printed wallpapers, stacks of hat-boxes and cigar-store figures. Mrs. Webb loved using brightly colored and patterned handmade quilts and coverlets for the beds, woven rag, braided and hooked rugs for the floors. As one of the earliest collectors of Americana, she admired the functional beauty found in

5

everyday objects, such as weathervanes, quilts and other textiles, shop and trade signs, tools, horse-drawn vehicles, furniture and decorative accessories.

Textiles became one of her main areas of collecting. Although Electra Webb initially collected quilts and other textiles for use and decoration in her home, she soon began to regard such pieces as works of art. She was attracted by the bold graphic patterns of pieced and appliquéd quilts, the clarity of line and shape found in elegant quilting and embroidery patterns, the strong geometric patterns of checked and plaid furnishing fabrics and overshot and doublecloth coverlets, the rich colors of whole-cloth wool quilts and the imaginative combinations of human figures, animals and vegetation—often whimsical and out-of-scale—found on quilts, embroideries and jacquard-woven coverlets.

On her death in 1960 Mrs. Webb bequeathed a collection of textiles to the Museum with a depth, range and quality found in few others. Assembled over a period of fifty years, the collection now includes quilts, coverlets, embroidered, woven, crocheted and knitted bedspreads and blankets, handwoven bedding and other household linens; printed and handwoven furnishing fabrics; hooked, woven, braided and embroidered rugs; and such decorative household accessories as samplers, pictorial embroidered and stumpwork pictures, beaded lambrequins and cushions.

The first building at the Shelburne Museum, the Horseshoe Barn, was built in 1947 to house the Webb family carriage collection. By 1952, the year the Museum opened to the public, the exhibits had grown to include a one-room schoolhouse, three completely furnished period homes, a seven-room inn, a covered bridge and a lighthouse. That same year Mrs. Webb began to plan an exhibit of quilts, textiles and woman's needle arts. In addition to fifty quilts from her personal collection, Mrs. Webb sought other textiles for the exhibit.

Family, friends, fellow collectors and antique dealers with whom Mrs. Webb had worked in the past all responded with pieces for this new project. Many of the quilts illustrated in this book came from that initial collecting effort. Florence Peto, the famous quilt author and collector, worked closely with Electra to help acquire such beautiful and unusual quilts as the Civil War Soldier quilt, Mariner's Compass with Hickory Leaf Medallion quilt and Framed Vase of Flowers counterpane. Mrs. Peto later worked with Museum staff to catalogue the collection. Elizabeth Spangler of Ephrata, Pennsylvania, who cultivated Electra's interest in handwoven coverlets, linens and yardage, located the Ohio and Evening Star quilt from central Pennsylvania; John K. Byard of Connecticut brought the Ann Robinson quilt to Electra's attention and Alice T. McLean contributed the Maryland Album quilt.

When first installed at the Shelburne Museum, the exhibition of more than 150 of Electra Webb's quilts and nearly 700 examples of textiles and accessories stirred a vast amount of interest. The quantity and variety of textiles on exhibit could not be seen anywhere else in the country. The display was revolutionary for the time; quilts were mounted on movable racks that visitors could turn like the pages of a book, while coverlets, textiles, costumes, rugs and accessories filled vitrines and cases throughout the eight-room, 1600-square-foot building. It was the first time a major American textile collection had been made so immediately accessible to the viewer. Today the latest conservation methods have been applied to Mrs. Webb's exhibit, but the basic presentation remains the same. The Museum maintains an exhibit of over one hundred quilts, rotating them from storage to exhibit on a regular basis to insure their preservation.

As visitors came to Shelburne and information about its wonderful collections spread, many people contacted the Museum about donations of important family heirlooms. Among the quilts selected for this volume, for example, Walter Kiggins of Manchester, Vermont, donated the Cory Presentation Album quilt made for his ancestor, Reverend Cory; Mrs. William Burton Westcott donated the Coxcomb quilt made by her mother, Edith Kingsley Stevens of Alburgh, Vermont; and recently, Ethel Washburn donated the Sunflower quilt made by her great-grandmother.

The scope of the quilt collection assembled by Electra Webb reflects the collecting interests of her generation. The types of quilts readily available at that time were primarily traditional patterns dating from the early through mid-nineteenth century from the New England states, New York, Pennsylvania, Maryland and New Jersey. The collection also is notable for its wide range of patterns. Many quilts were acquired because they were unique additions to the collection. The correspondence for one textile explains it was purchased by Mrs. Webb because "we do not have an example of that pattern."

Like many collectors active from the 1920s through the 1950s, Mrs. Webb did not favor late nineteenth-century and early twentieth-century quilts. She was less interested in textiles of her own generation than those created at an earlier time. Mrs. Webb and other museum builders of her time such as Henry Ford, Henry Francis Dupont, Henry and Katherine Flint and Katherine Prentis Murphy focused their collecting activities on antiques that matched their vision of early American life.

In the 1950s few people collected quilts and even fewer on the scale of Electra Webb. A great deal of material remained in private hands and family collections. Florence Peto, in her book *Historic Quilts*, published in 1935, mentions the rarity of embroidery wool blankets, pieces that we know now are not rare but at that time were still undiscovered. Victorian crazy quilts, Art Nouveau and Art Deco quilts, regional Amish, Midwestern and Hawaiian examples were not represented in Electra's collection because of their relative non-antique status or unavailability during the time she was collecting. However, subsequent donations and purchases have broadened the Shelburne collection. Several Hawaiian quilts were donated in the 1960s by George Frelinghuysen, and in 1967 Mrs. Webb's son, J. Watson Webb, Jr., donated the Museum's first Amish quilt. Recently a number of important Amish quilts were added to the collection as well as a Kentucky signature quilt and a North Dakota Star of Bethlehem.

The Shelburne quilt collection now numbers more than 400 examples, dating from the late eighteenth to the mid-twentieth centuries and representing a wide range of styles and techniques. The quilts illustrated in this book cover the range of the collection: whole-cloth quilts made with wool or printed cottons, quilts with elaborate quilted patterns, intricately pieced quilts of geometric patterns or pieced floral patterns, early broderie perse and mid-nineteenth-century appliqué quilts, elaborately patterned and pictorial appliqué quilts, late nineteenth-century log cabin and crazy quilts and twentieth-century quilts with traditional patterns as well as those with contemporary colors and patterns.

Each quilt has at least one unique quality to recommend its place in the collection: the quality of needlework, choice of materials, overall beauty, original condition, history of manufacture and/or history of ownership, rarity, pattern or design. The Museum continues to acquire outstanding and well-documented quilts to further develop the collection.

The Shelburne Museum, often known as a "collection of collections," is located on the shores of Lake Champlain in northwestern Vermont. It is home to world-renowned collections of American folk art including weathervanes, decoys, carousel animals, cigar-store figures, trade signs, scrimshaw, ship carvings, painted furniture, coverlets and, of course, quilts. There also are extensive collections of toys, dolls, carriages, tools and American and European paintings. The collections are exhibited in 37 historic structures and buildings set in a 45-acre park of manicured lawns, roses, lilacs, apple trees and formal gardens. The Museum is open daily from mid-May to mid-October and by appointment the rest of the year.

LIST OF PLATES

ALPHABETICAL LIST OF QUILTS

Commemorative Textile Quilt, front pieced, maker and origin unknown, printed cotton handkerchief and flags, c. 1876–1880s (94″ × 89″)
GIFT OF J. WATSON WEBB, JR.

In 1876 an International Centennial Exposition was held in Philadelphia to commemorate the one hundredth anniversary of the United States as a free nation. This event was popularized in magazines, lithographs, games, toys and printed and woven textiles of the time. The central panel of this quilt features commemorative textiles illustrating the Memorial Hall Art Gallery and other exhibition structures. Other subjects illustrated are the Declaration of Independence and the flags and shields of the nations participating in the Exposition.

Commemorative Textile Quilt, verso, whole cloth and pieced, cotton

The reverse of the quilt illustrated opposite is made primarily of one piece of fabric, known as a "cheater" print, which imitates or creates the illusion of a pieced quilt. At some point during its history, the quilt was cut to fit a four-post bed, and a later owner filled the voids with printed textiles unrelated to the general theme.

Broken Star Quilt, pieced and quilted, maker unkown, Holmes County, Ohio, cotton, c. 1920s (90″ × 86″)

Patterns based on heavenly bodies such as the sun and stars are common in Amish quilting and are found in both Eastern and Midwestern quilts. With a large central star enclosed by a pieced border, the Broken Star is one of the most dramatic star patterns. The sharp contrast of the black background and the brightly colored pieced pattern adds to the effect of the overall design. This elaborately pieced design is assembled from the usual geometric shapes: squares, rectangles, diamonds and triangles. The background is filled with quilting in more representational designs: feathers, waffles, flowers and medallions.

Tumbling Block Star Quilt, pieced and quilted, maker unknown, Lancaster County, Pennsylvania, wool, c. 1890s (98″ × 66″)

Patterns used by the Amish quiltmakers of Lancaster County typically incorporate more subdued color schemes than those of communities later established in the Midwest. The predominant use of black for adult Amish and Mennonite clothes made it an obvious choice for background color, and it is not unusual to see several shades of black in a quilt top. Most Amish patterns, including this Tumbling Block Star, could be pieced from sewing fabric scraps. Judging by the small pieces making up this pattern, the several shades of black and the somber colors, it is likely this quilt was made from leftover fabric—a reflection of a frugal lifestyle.

See the Frontispiece (p. 2) and its caption (p. 4) for further background on Amish quilts.

Railroad Crossing Quilt, pieced and quilted, maker unknown, Holmes County, Ohio, cotton, c. 1930s (80″ × 80″)

Amish and Mennonite communities in the Midwest are often widely separated, so Amish visit more with their "English" (non-Amish) neighbors than they would in the East. Influenced by this contact, quilters often use a greater variety of patterns and incorporate "English" ideas into their traditional patterns, making them freer in design and use of color. The Railroad Crossing pattern was widely used by Midwestern Amish, and this example illustrates the brighter and more varied color schemes found in both their clothing and their quilts. The combination of pinks, yellow, orange, blue and turquoise is not unusual for a Midwestern quilt.

Abstract Diamond Crib Quilt, pieced and quilted, maker unknown, Kansas, cotton, c. 1915 (55″ × 49″)

Although Amish quilts are today regarded as art objects, their makers intended them only as warm bedcovers for their families. The Amish tradition combines a love of beauty and high-quality craftsmanship. The exact patterns of the quilts, finely stitched seams and precisely executed quilting attest to their makers' high level of skill. This quilt is made of readily available fabric scraps, but the simplicity of the pattern, the seemingly random pieced diamonds, the subtle colors and the quilted designs produce an abstract and dramatic effect.

15

Joseph's Coat Quilt, pieced and quilted, maker unknown, Lancaster County, Pennsylvania, cotton, c. 1920s (81" × 76")

Few quilts are as dramatic as this classic Mennonite Joseph's Coat with its bold use of color. The Mennonites used bright colors for children's clothes and men's shirts including yellow, red, orange, purple, mauve, turquoise, magenta, gold and green. Shades of blue, brown, tan and gray were also used. All were recycled into quilts. The simple stripe pattern is enhanced by quilting each strip in a different pattern including diamonds, cables, vines and scrolls.

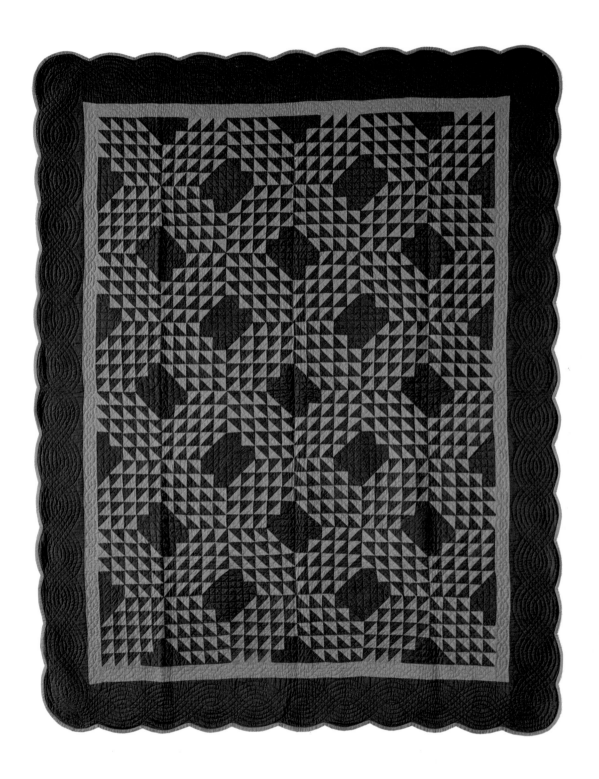

Ocean Waves Quilt, pieced and quilted, maker unknown, Ohio, cotton, c. 1930s (88″ × 86″)

The Ocean Waves pattern is frequently used by Amish quilters in the Midwest and reflects the departure from traditional patterns seen in quilts from this area resulting from increased contact with non-Amish neighbors. Although the pattern is often worked in a varied color scheme, this quilter limited herself to two colors, creating a simple yet elegant quilt enhanced by the scalloped border and the cable, wave and diamond quilting patterns.

Abraham Lincoln Presentation Counterpane, appliqué and pieced, cotton, maker and origin unknown, dated 1865 (83½″ × 78″)

This presentation quilt is made of 49 squares, each appliquéd, pieced or embroidered with a different pattern and signed by the maker. One of the makers initialed her square "L.V." and dated it "Feb. 10th, 1865." Presentation or album quilts were often made to commemorate a special event such as a retirement, anniversary or parting. The quiltmakers often designed blocks with images of personal significance: in this example, a house, anchor, family Bible and a man training a mule. Two of the most interesting blocks represent Abraham Lincoln. The first, probably copied from a printed illustration, depicts the President sitting in an armchair, and the second and more imaginative depicts the Lincoln-Douglas debates.

Centennial Album Quilt, appliqué, made by members of the Burdick-Childs family, North Adams, Massachusetts, cotton, c. 1876–1880s (78½″ × 79¼″)

At least three of the 36 blocks in this quilt were inspired by the American Centennial Celebration of 1876, as depictions include Memorial Hall, the streets of Philadelphia and banners reading ''Declaration of Independence . . . Centennial Anniversary . . . 1776 . . . 1876.'' Others illustrate family, friends, home, biblical and popular events. The blocks entitled ''My first proposal,'' ''My last proposal'' and ''The Tiresome Boy'' are tributes to the maker's sense of humor. The fabrics were chosen to emphasize such details as landscape, architectural features and building materials. It is likely that one person designed and made most of the blocks while other less skilled family members contributed the rest.

Major Ringgold Album Quilt, appliqué, pieced and quilted, maker unknown, Baltimore, Maryland, cotton, c. 1846–1850s (110″ × 94″)

Baltimore-style album quilts, made by professional quiltmakers and imitated by skilled amateurs, are known for the excellence of their craftsmanship, their use of a wide range of elaborate textiles and the overall harmony of their design. As the second largest port in America during the mid-nineteenth century, Baltimore was a major trade center and beautifully printed and woven fabrics were widely available. Quiltmakers took advantage of this opportunity to purchase a variety of fabrics and skillfully used them in multilayer appliqué to emphasize their designs. The Ringgold monument and eagles are made from the popular rainbow fabrics, which were often used for realistic shading and texture. Many Baltimore-style quilts commemorate events and heroes of earlier wars. Major Ringgold, a native of Baltimore and a little-known hero of the 1846 Battle of Palo Alto, was one of the first Americans to die in the war with Mexico.

Maryland Album Quilt, appliqué, pieced and quilted, maker unknown, Maryland, cotton, c. 1840–1850s (101″ × 98″)

This quilt was probably made to imitate the elaborate Baltimore album quilts of the same period. The maker incorporated the block design and appliqué motifs found in Baltimore album quilts, including floral wreaths, bouquets and baskets. This quilt was the cherished possession of the previous owner's family, and when entered in the Maryland State Fair and Agricultural Society in 1939, won first prize in the Household Department. State and county agricultural societies often sponsored agricultural fairs featuring farm produce, baked goods and domestically produced textiles and fancywork. Prizes were offered and a list of the premium winners published in the local newspapers. This practice continues today in some rural areas.

Ann Robinson Counterpane, appliqué and embroidered, made by Ann Robinson, possibly Connecticut, cotton and linen, dated "October 1ˢᵗ 1813 . . . Finished January 27ᵗʰ 1814" (100" × 95")

The elaborate appliqué and patterning found in this counterpane by Ann Robinson illustrate the popularity of appliqué work in American quilts after 1800. Many of the designs relate to other needlework traditions. The two trees or shrubs at the base of the quilt appear to be stylized trees of life inspired by Indian textiles, while the animals running over the mounds relate to needlework samplers. Jane Nylander, in her research on early New England quilts, pointed out the similarity in overall design and some of the individual motifs to the Greenfield Hill quilt also from Connecticut and formerly in the Henry Ford Museum collection.

Mary Jane Carr Counterpane, appliqué and embroidered, Mary Jane Carr, Columbia, Lancaster County, Pennsylvania, cotton, silk velvet, wool yarn, dated 1854 (99″ × 92″)
GIFT OF ELECTRA H. WEBB

This quilt combines the framed medallion design popular earlier in the century with a variety of appliqué motifs. Each of the eight triangles contains different patterns and the quiltmaker incorporated a variety of needlework techniques to highlight her designs. Many of the flowers and leaves are outlined in yarn and decorated with braid and yarn. Chintz cutouts are used for flowers, and scraps of velvet for fruit and leaves. The quilt is signed in cross-stitch: "Mary Jane Carr's Quilt Completed in 1854."

Framed Vase of Flowers Counterpane, reverse appliqué, pieced and quilted, made by a member of the Dumont family, Mobile, Alabama, cotton and linen, c. 1800–1820s (101″ × 86″)
GIFT OF FLORENCE PETO

Many design motifs, such as flowering urns and vases and exotic birds, were introduced to English and American needlework patterns from Indian textiles. The central motif is made in reverse appliqué with small button-like decorations created by shirring a circle, drawing the thread tight and tacking the fabric in place on the ground. The textiles used in this early quilt include handwoven linen as well as block- and roller-printed linen and cotton.

Flower Basket Counterpane, reverse appliqué, maker unknown, possibly Pennsylvania, cotton, c. 1820–1840s (76″ × 76″)
GIFT OF MRS. JOHN WILMERDING

This large, elaborate basket of blossoms, with its lacy and delicate flowers and foliage framed by curving vines, resembles a pattern more often used on small pictorial embroidery work than on a full-size bedcover. All design motifs are worked in reverse appliqué, a complex technique used by skilled quilters. The plain fabric ground is laid over the printed fabric planned for the pattern areas. The top fabric is cut away along penciled pattern lines, and then the rough edges are turned under and hemmed to reveal the printed fabric below.

*Broderie Perse Tree of Life Counterpane, appliqué and pieced, maker and location
unknown, cotton and linen, c. 1790–1810s (106″ × 103″)*
GIFT OF ELECTRA H. WEBB

By 1800, the broderie perse technique was extremely popular with American
quilters. Motifs were cut from printed fabrics and applied to a solid ground of linen
or cotton. The makers of broderie perse quilts often enhanced their creations with
embroidery or other needlework. Ink was used for detail and later for inscriptions.
The image of a central tree covered with flowers and birds illustrates the biblical
Tree of Life, one of the forbidden trees in the Garden of Eden, which conferred
immortality on those who ate the fruit (Genesis ii:9). This motif enjoyed long
popularity in European and American textiles.

Tree of Life Quilt, appliqué and quilted, made by Sarah T. C. H. Miller, location unknown, cotton, dated 1830s (125″ × 109″)

Elaborate chintz quilts and counterpanes were made predominantly in the eastern and southern United States. Products of an affluent society, they were intended not for warmth, but for decoration. Quilters usually cut the individual printed designs from yards of expensive chintz fabric and appliquéd them to a plain ground, a variation of the broderie perse or "Persian embroidery" technique. Many of the appliqué chintz quilts of this type feature a tree of life as the central motif. In her quilt, Sarah T. C. H. Miller substituted a stand of double and single hollyhocks and aster-like flowers.

*Fox and Geese Medallion Quilt, reverse appliqué, pieced and trapunto, maker and
location unknown, cotton and linen, c. 1820–1840s (103″ × 100″)*
GIFT OF DUNDEEN BOSTWICK

Leafy fronds were used originally to surround portraits and coats of arms as an
emblem of honor. In this quilt the fronds enclose a trapunto vase of flowers. The
Wild Goose Chase pieced bands and trailing vine border of this quilt provide a
dramatic frame for the center motif. All pattern motifs are worked in reverse
appliqué and the white areas of the field are filled with small trapunto figures.
Fabrics used include various roller-printed cottons popular at this time.

Medallion Block Quilt, pieced, embroidered and quilted, maker unknown, Connecticut, wool and wool yarns, c. 1820–1840s (88" × 84")

The design of this quilt appears to be an interesting combination of the early framed medallion style adopted from English needlework traditions and block piecing developed in America. This entire quilt is made of a variety of woolen fabric in plain and twill weaves of different weights. The blocks are embroidered with different floral motifs in singles and two-ply wool thread. The quilt is backed with handwoven linen plain-weave fabric similar to sheeting.

Chintz Album Counterpane, appliqué, maker unknown, southern United States, cotton, c. 1840–1850 (112" × 109")

During the mid-nineteenth century, women would often request quilt blocks made and signed by their friends and relatives to be joined together in album quilts. The blocks of this quilt date over a range of years and were apparently acquired by one person and then made into a quilt; the inscriptions read: "To Mother 1854," "Mother from Sue 1855," "Sister Polly from Mary" and "To my cousin Mary from R.I.W. 1850." The quilt was passed down through a New England family and carefully preserved, but was never used because the family was rather ashamed that it had been stolen by the great-grandfather from a southern mansion during the Civil War when his New Hampshire regiment fought nearby.

Cory Presentation Album Quilt, appliqué and quilted, made by members of the Presbyterian Church, Perth Amboy, New Jersey, cotton, dated 1852–1853 (93″ × 93½″)
GIFT OF WALTER KIGGINS

In 1852, Reverend Cory announced to his congregation that he was retiring after twenty years of ministry. In recognition of his long service and friendship, his parishioners created this album quilt, which they presented to Rev. Cory and his wife. Each of the 121 blocks is signed by its maker and almost every one contains a biblical passage or verse from a psalm. Many of the blocks are dated, confirming that the quilt was made in 1852 and 1853. Each contributor appliquéd floral designs cut from glazed chintz fabric to an 8½″ square of fine white cotton. The completed blocks were sewn together, attached to a cotton backing and quilted along the seam lines in a tulip pattern.

Rose of Sharon Quilt, appliqué and quilted, made by Sarah Barber, Waterville, Vermont, cotton, c. 1840–1850s (90″ × 85″)
<small>GIFT OF MRS. RUPERT KING</small>

The variety of rose patterns that appear in mid-nineteenth-century quilts attests to their popularity. The basic Rose of Sharon pattern consists of one large blossom surrounded by buds on a single stalk. Quilters used a variety of borders to complete their quilts; here, the swag and tassel border provides an elegant frame for the floral blocks. By stuffing the central flower and rose buds heavily to create a three-dimensional effect, Sarah Barber worked a masterpiece.

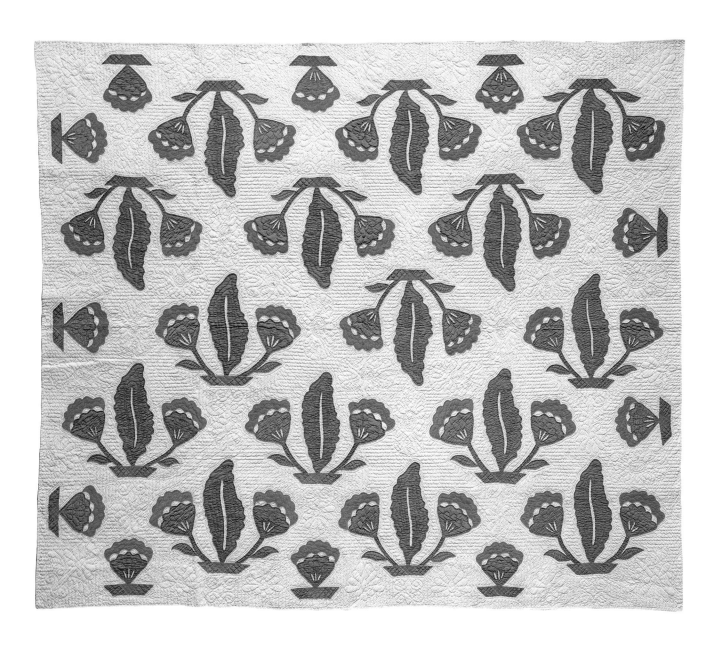

*Coxcomb Quilt, appliqué and quilted, made by Edith Kingsley Stevens, Alburgh,
Vermont, cotton, c. 1900–1930s (93″ × 80″)*
GIFT OF MRS. WILLIAM BURTON WESCOTT

This quilt was made in Alburgh, Vermont, a small community on Lake Champlain
neaer the Canadian border, around the turn of the twentieth century. Mrs. Edith
Kingsley Stevens was born August 5, 1879 and taught school in Alburgh until her
marriage in the late 1890s. She appliquéd the pattern pieces and, with other female
members of the family, quilted the layers together on a frame on the second floor of
her home. After her death in 1946, the quilt passed to her daughter, who in turn gave
it to the Shelburne Museum.

Sunflower Quilt, appliqué and quilted, made by Carrie M. Carpenter, Northfield, Vermont, cotton, c. 1860s (84" × 75")
GIFT OF ETHEL WASHBURN

We know little of Carrie Carpenter's life in Northfield, a small town in north-central Vermont, but she must have been an avid gardener to design and appliqué these three marvelous sunflower plants growing up from the base of her quilt. The leaves and petals are cut from solid-colored fabrics, and brown calico print was used in the center of the blossoms to simulate seed pods. The stalks are lightly stuffed and the leaves are quilted in matching green thread to give some depth to the textile. Brown thread is used for the diamond quilting pattern on the seeds.

Bias Pomegranate Quilt, appliqué and quilted, maker and location unknown, cotton, c. 1840–1860s (83″ × 82″)
GIFT OF ELECTRA H. WEBB

While pomegranates and trailing vines were often-used motifs in mid-nineteenth-century appliqué quilts, rarely were they incorporated into so bold an overall design as in these broad bias strips. The quilt stitches are exceptionally fine and outline the appliqué to highlight the pattern. Other motifs, including curled feathers, eight-pointed stars and hearts, are randomly quilted on the white ground.

*Oak Leaves and Orange Slices Counterpane, appiqué and pieced, maker unknown,
New England, cotton, c. 1840–1860s (109″ × 89¾″)*
GIFT OF RICHARD GIPSON AND ROGER WENTWORTH

While women of previous generations spent hours producing cloth for household
linens and textiles, women in the mid-nineteenth century were able to obtain a wide
variety of fabric produced by mills. Consequently their time freed from the looms
could be spent on a variety of sewing and needlework, especially quilts. The large
amounts of fabric required for this quilt and the subtle variations in chintz prints
indicate that the fabric was purchased expressly for this quilt. Each of the blocks is
cut in a variation of the oak leaf, reel and orange slice pattern. These popular
quilting patterns were used by themselves or combined with other motifs to create a
unique design.

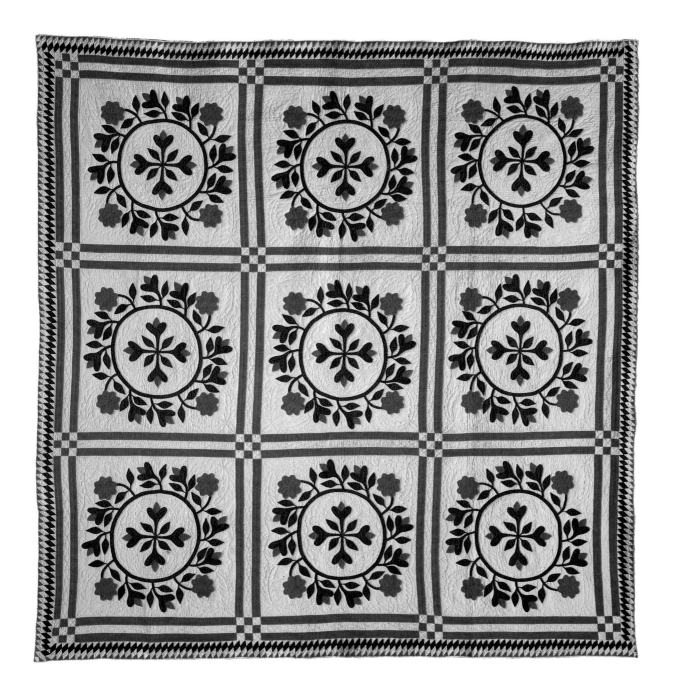

Presidential Wreath Quilt, appliqué, pieced and quilted, made by members of the Traver family, Sand Lake, New York, cotton, c. 1845–1850s (96″ × 96″)
GIFT OF KITTY WEBB HARRIS

The Presidential wreath pattern, which originated in New Jersey, was probably inspired by an 1845 Currier & Ives lithograph commemorating George Washington's inaugural parade in April 1789. The print, entitled "Washington's Reception by the Ladies . . . , on passing the bridges at Trenton, NJ . . . ," depicts women with rose wreaths in their hair strewing blossoms in front of Washington's procession along streets decorated with rose garlands. This elegant pattern is a wonderful example of the way in which a skilled quilter combines very simple design devices to create a masterpiece. Two solid colors contrast with the white ground, which is filled with quilted designs highlighting the appliquéd motifs. The striped sashing is punctuated by nine-patch corners and an intricate sawtooth border.

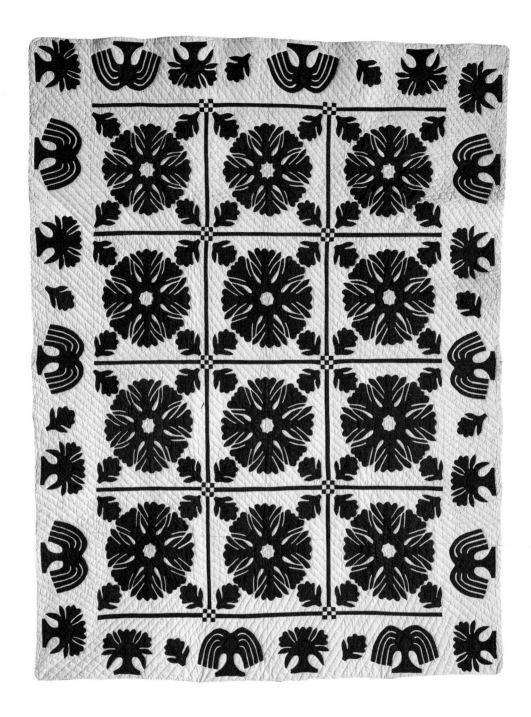

Snowflake Medallion and Willow Border Quilt, appliqué, pieced and quilted, maker unknown, possibly Boston, Massachusetts, cotton, c. 1840–1850s (92" × 72")

In the mid-nineteenth century, many quilts were made with the pattern motifs cut of one solid color set against a white ground. The overall design of this quilt, with the abstract snowflake pattern in the center field and willow tree border, relates to the bold medallion pattern used on jacquard-woven coverlets popular in the same period. Mid-nineteenth-century jacquard coverlets were typically woven in white and one other color, often dark blue. The popularity of these "fancy coverlets," as they were advertised, might have prompted a taste for similarly designed quilts. The previous owner stated: "[the quilt] was made in Boston on Beacon Street . . . [and was found] wrapped in a handwoven sheet and a newspaper dated 1861 . . . packed away in a chest."

Mariner's Compass with Hickory Leaf Medallion Quilt, pieced, appliqué and quilted, maker unknown, possibly New Jersey, cotton, c. 1830–1840s (100″ × 96″)

Pieced quilts were at their zenith in the mid-nineteenth century and quilters went to great lengths to outdo one another in design and workmanship. The pieced compass designs here are set off brilliantly by the delicate hickory-leaf-and-orange-slice design. Great skill was required to piece the tapered points of the Mariner's Compass pattern. All geometric piecing demands neatness with even, well-defined points and angles. To assure accuracy and an even edge, small pieces were often basted to a paper lining. The diamond-quilted compass centers are repeated in the center of the appliqué motif, and the Persian-pear print border fabric is quilted in the diamond-chain design.

Virginia Lily Quilt, pieced and appliqué, and quilted, maker and location unknown, cotton, c. 1840–1860s (91½" × 89¾")

The block style of quilting worked with individually pieced or appliquéd squares is uniquely American. The general construction of this quilt is typical of other block designs in that the quilter pieced and appliquéd each block separately before sewing them together. Yet when finishing this quilt, the maker treated the center field as if it were a length of fabric and attached the border to cut the flower patterns in half at the sides and bottom. The lily pattern, which typically groups the flower in threes, has many variations, each known by a different name such as Day Lily, Meadow Lily or Virginia Lily.

Tulip and Orange Slices Quilt, appliqué, pieced and quilted, maker unknown, Kingston, Massachusetts, cotton, c. 1840–1860s (95″ × 94″)

When set on the ground fabric, some appliqué patterns create an overall design with a very different effect. In this quilt the tulip leaves, or so-called orange slices, form a latticework or sashing that separates and frames the tulip-flower heads and the medallions at the base of the stems. The white ground area by the leaves is filled with quilted feathered scrolls and flower sprays. The unusual scalloped edge trimmed in red, the pieced ribbon band and the quilted trailing grapevine provide an elegant border for the quilt.

ABOVE:

Civil War Soldier Quilt, appliqué, pieced and quilted, maker unknown, northeastern United States, cotton, c. 1860–1870s (112″ × 96″)
GIFT OF FLORENCE PETO

This quilt is believed to have been made by a Civil War soldier recuperating from his injuries. The motifs incorporated into the design certainly give credibility to the story: armed soldiers on horseback and on foot march in file along the border, while the center medallion is filled with more marching soldiers and female figures possibly depicting nurses carrying food trays. The female figure was probably copied from the trademark of Baker's Chocolate, which in turn was copied from Jean-Etienne Liotard's (1702–1789) pastel entitled *La Belle Chocolatière,* now in the Staatliche Kunstsammlungen, Dresden, East Germany. The intricate mosaic piecework of the two intermediate borders strengthens the framed medallion composition of the quilt.

OPPOSITE:

Calico Garden Quilt, pieced, appliqué and quilted, made by Florence Peto, New Jersey, cotton, c. 1950s (49″ × 39″)
GIFT OF FLORENCE PETO

Florence Peto (1884–1970), the noted quilt collector and author, often made quilts using scraps of antique fabric. This crib quilt, named "Calico Garden" by the maker, incorporates many eighteenth- and nineteenth-century hand-blocked and copperplate prints, chintzes and English and French calicos. Many of the individual flower blossoms are worked in the broderie perse technique, in which flower motifs were cut from a printed textile and appliquéd to the quilt background (see pages 26 and 27). Mrs. Peto and Electra Havemeyer Webb, the founder of the Shelburne Museum, were great friends and worked together to build the Shelburne quilt collection.

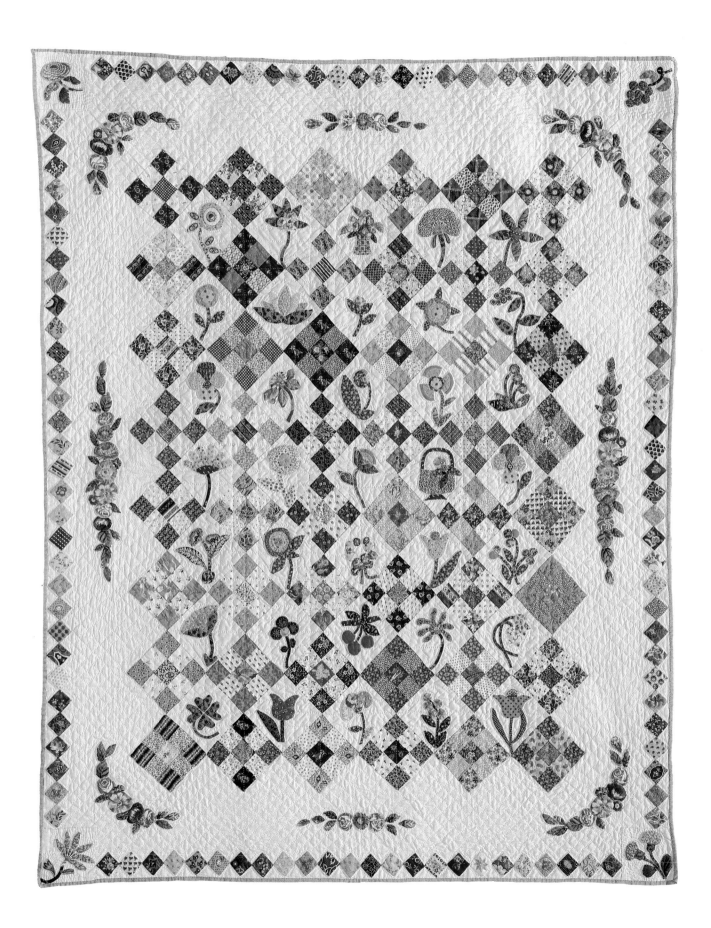

Fruit Basket Quilt, pieced, appliqué and quilted, maker unknown, Pennsylvania, cotton, c. 1840–1806s (83″ × 72½″)

Fruit- and flower-filled baskets were popular patterns for both pieced and appliquéd quilts in the mid- to late nineteenth century. This popularity probably relates to both their historic use as a needlework motif and the study of botany as a suitable pastime for nineteenth-century women. Although the maker of this quilt chose a much-used pattern, she made it unique by filling the baskets with trapunto stuffed fruit and setting the individual pattern blocks in a diagonal design divided by triple sashing. The use of three very strong colors adds to the dramatic effect of this design.

*Feathered Star and Oak Leaves Quilt, pieced, appliqué and quilted, made by Mary
A. Purdy, Springfield Center, New York, cotton, dated [June 18] 1869 (90″ × 74″)*

The feathered-star pattern is usually worked with the plain white areas filled with
quilting. Mary Purdy, however, decided to scatter the oak leaves, a symbol of
remembrance and longevity, used in the border over the entire quilt. The oak-leaf
vine was appliquéd after the pieced center field was completed, as the leaves extend
onto the pieced blocks. The bright yellow and green print used for the leaves
provides a sharp contrast to the brown stars. The intricate pieced edges of the
feathered star are emphasized by the lines quilted across the stars and the white
areas. The black ink used to sign and date the quilt has blurred, leaving only the
name and year clearly legible.

*Eagle and Shield Quilt, appliqué, pieced and quilted, made by Lydia Stafford,
Vermont, cotton, c. 1830–1840s (100″ × 84″)*

The American bald eagle, adopted as the national symbol in 1782, appeared in
American decoration as early as 1776. George Washington commissioned a dining-
room carpet featuring the American eagle, and a description appeared in the
Literary Repository of 1791, "holding in his dexter an olive branch . . . in his
sinister a bundle of thirteen arrows" (representing the original thirteen colonies)
and "in his beak, a scroll inscribed with the motto E Pluribus Unum." Although
family tradition relates that Lydia Stafford made this quilt for her hope chest before
she married Warren Barstowe on his return from the War of 1812, the appliqué
block style of the quilt suggests that it was made later in the nineteenth century.

Hawaiian Quilt, appliqué and quilted, maker unknown, Hawaii, cotton, c. 1900 (78½″ × 75″)

North Americans first began residing in Hawaii in the 1820s to trade textiles and other goods for the native sandalwood and to convert the Polynesians to Christianity. Missionary women also taught the Hawaiians a variety of sewing and needlework skills including quilting. By the late nineteenth century a distinct Hawaiian quilt style had evolved. It combined pieced and appliqué quilting traditions with Hawaiian tapa-cloth bedcovers made with stamped and incised designs. A solid-color fabric, folded and cut like a child's paper snowflake, was appliquéd onto a solid, usually white, background fabric. The top was then quilted to a lining and backing; the quilting stitches usually repeated the appliqué design. Because of the mild tropical climate, these elaborate bedcovers were used more for decoration than for warmth.

Star of Bethlehem Quilt, pieced and quilted, made by Mrs. Marie Marin, St. Pie,
Quebec, Canada, wool, c. 1860–1880s (73″ × 71½″)
GIFT OF LILIAN B. CARLISLE

Experienced quilters knew how the use of different fabrics and colors changed the
effect of the design. The often-used central-star pattern, made entirely of diamond-
shaped pieces, was generally worked in printed or solid-color cottons, but the effect
produced by the use of solid-color wool fabrics is entirely different. Much of the
fabric used in this quilt was handwoven and dyed by the maker, Mrs. Marie (Emile)
Marin (1820s–1902). Mrs. Marin, who made this quilt before she moved to Vermont,
raised fourteen children. Her daughter-in-law, the donor, remembered her weaving
and dyeing cloth to be used for household textiles and clothing.

*Star of Bethlehem Quilt, pieced and appliqué, made by a member of the Sioux tribe,
North Dakota, cotton, c. 1900s (78″ × 70″)*
GIFT OF JOHN WILMERDING

Quilting was not a traditional American Indian needleworking technique, and
Indian-made quilts do not begin to appear until the late nineteenth century. The
floral corner blocks of this quilt are similar in style to patterns used in Sioux
beadwork. All piecing and quilting was done by hand, even though this quilt dates
from the turn of the century when sewing machines were widely available in most
parts of the United States. Only the narrow pink binding was sewn by machine.

Triple Irish Chain Quilt, pieced and quilted, made by Margie Gorrecht, York County, Pennsylvania, cotton, c. 1840–1860s (100″ × 92″)

The Irish-chain pattern, popular in both England and America, was made in single-, double- and triple-chain variations. The basic geometric pattern is elegant in its simplicity. The neutral areas provided a skilled needleworker with large spaces for quilted designs. Margie Gorrecht worked feathered wreaths in the squares and a winding plume with maple leaves and tulips along the border.

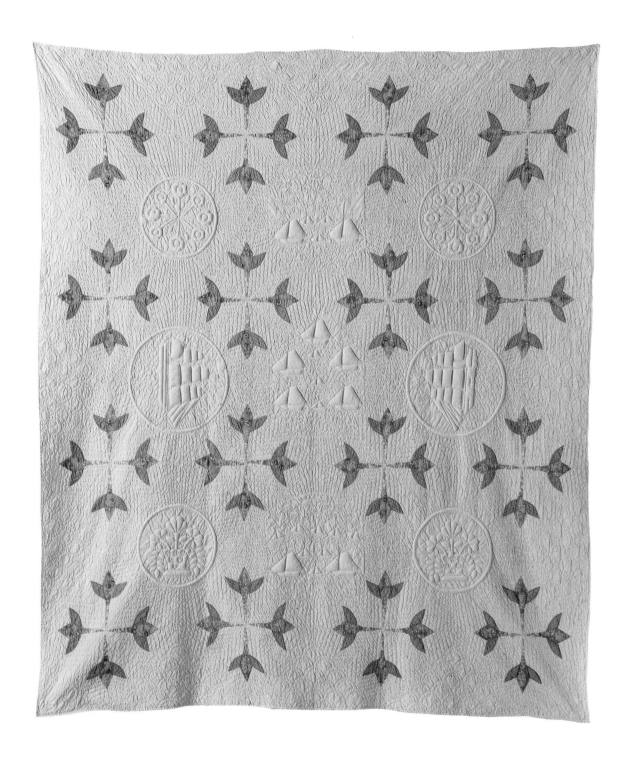

Trilobe Flowers and Clipper Ships Quilt, pieced, quilted and trapunto, maker unknown, coastal New England, cotton, c. 1840s–1850s (89″ × 68″)
GIFT OF ELECTRA H. WEBB

While the color interest in this quilt is created by the sixteen groups of crossed trilobe flowers, the design interest is in the trapunto sailing ships and potted flowers that fill the negative spaces of the quilt. Trapunto or stuffed work is made by first stitching the outline of the quilting design through all layers of the quilt where the padding is desired. The quilter then stuffs a cotton filling through a tiny opening in the backing fabric within the quilted area, creating a puffed, three-dimensional effect on the surface of the quilt.

Spatterwork and Triangle Mosaic Quilt, pieced and painted, made by "R.S.B.,"
location unknown, cotton, c. 1880–1900 (88½" × 87")

During the nineteenth century, spatterwork appeared as a surface decoration on
ceramics, occasionally on floors but rarely on textiles. The spatterwork designs on
this quilt were probably created by laying a paper template on the fabric surface and
using an atomizer to spray the fabric with ink or thinned paint. Dried ferns and
flowers were also used as patterns. Such fine details as feathers, flower petals and
leaves were added later with a fine brush or pen. The mosaic-pattern pieced blocks
provide a strong visual contrast.

Mountain Landscape Quilt, appliqué and quilted, maker unknown, northern New York, cotton, c. 1920–1930 (91½″ × 77″)
GIFT OF GEORGE FRELINGHUYSEN

Quilts that translate a favorite scene into a textile painting are rare and highly prized. The quality of work and attention to detail marks this quilt as the product of a highly skilled, experienced and sophisticated craftsperson. Various aspects of the scene are emphasized by stitching, including the sky, the snow-covered mountains and the individual logs in the cabin. The quilt has never been washed, and thus retains the original glaze on the fabrics as well as the pencil marks made by the quilter.

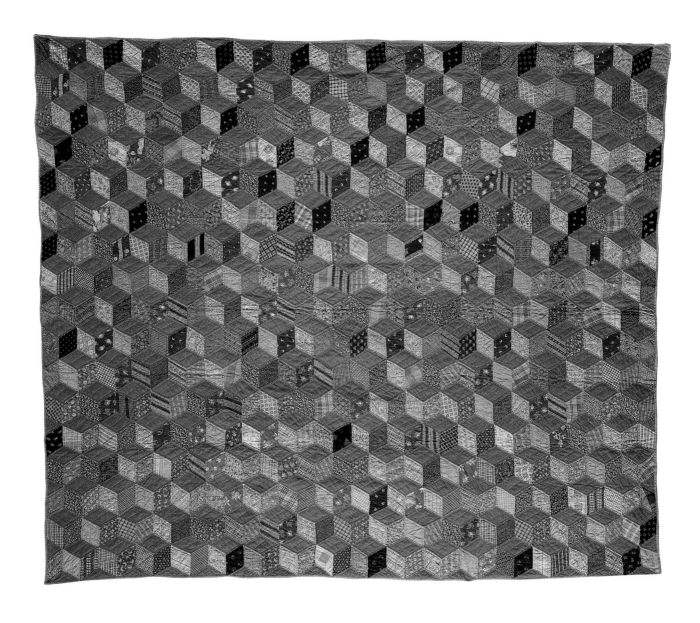

Box Quilt, pieced, made by Sarah Weir Ely, New England, cotton, c. 1880s (83″ × 70″)

The box pattern is based on diamond shapes of contrasting light and dark fabric pieced together to create a continuous three-dimensional stairlike design. The pattern has many names, among them Stair Steps, Diamonds, Box Patchwork and Baby Blocks. Popular quilt patterns were often used for other household items. In the June 1852 *Godey's Lady's Book,* instructions are given for making a "Mouchoir Case for Handkerchiefs" in the box pattern. This quilt exhibits the range and wealth of fabrics available to the late-nineteenth-century quiltmaker. One piece of fabric is documented as having been made by the Cocheco Print Works of Dover, New Hampshire Style #1082, July 6, 1884.

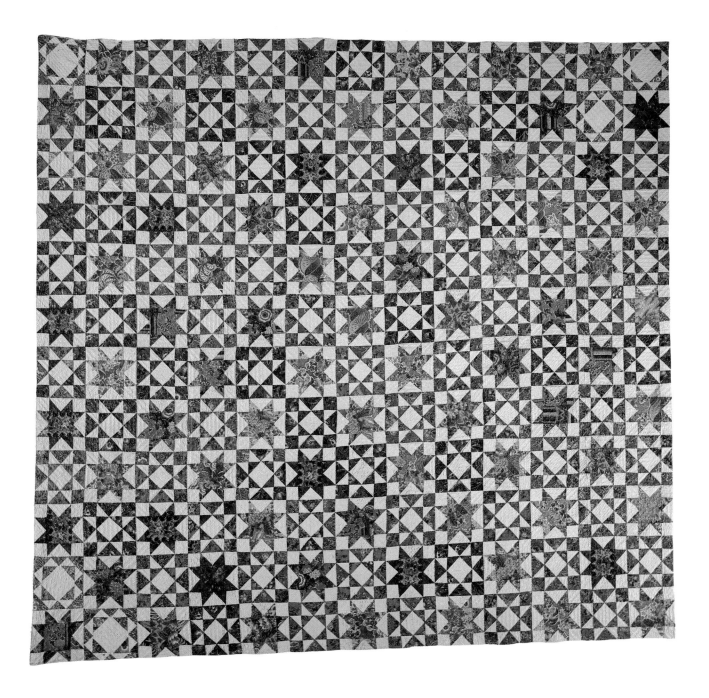

Ohio and Evening Star Quilt, pieced and quilted, made by "E.L.H.," Lancaster County, Pennsylvania, cotton, dated 1839 (123½″ × 114″)

Star quilts are made in innumerable variations such as Morning Star, Ohio Star, Evening Star, Lemoyne Star and Variable Star. This pattern is based on squares used whole and divided into equal right triangles. Four blocks in the quilt are deliberately made in another pattern. Supposedly some quiltmakers believed that only God could achieve perfection and it was presumptuous of mortals to try. Consequently, these quilters incorporated a deliberate "error" into their finished quilt. The date and maker's initials are worked in cross-stitch on the lining of this quilt.

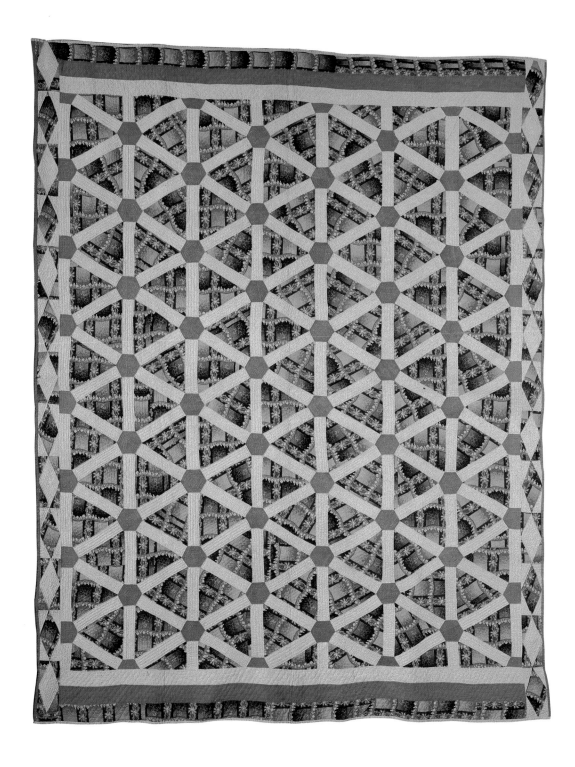

Hexagon and Triangle Quilt, pieced and quilted, maker and location unknown, cotton, c. 1850s (97" × 76")
GIFT OF ELECTRA H. WEBB

The strong use of colors in printed and solid-color fabrics in this quilt creates a three-dimensional appearance. The rainbow or ombre printing technique was used first to print wallpapers around 1826. But by 1846, reference is made to the availability of rainbow-printed fabrics. The printer obtained a rainbow of different colors or a range of intensity in one color on a length of fabric by gradually shading the ink colors on the print roller. The design could be varied by blending one color smoothly to the next or by incorporating ripples or zigzag effects.

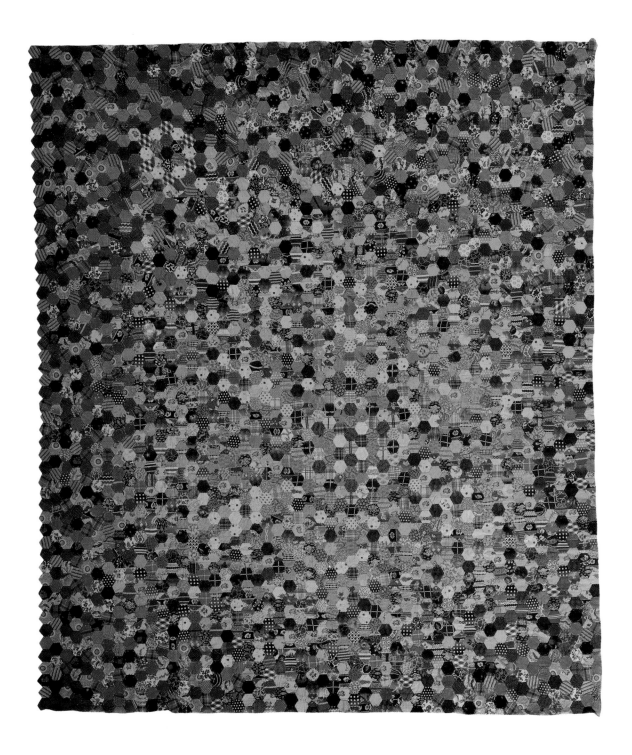

*Hexagon Mosaic Counterpane, pieced, maker unknown, England and Pennsyl-
vania, wool, cotton, paper, c. 1840–1850s (78½″ × 67¼″)*
Gift of Mrs. Edith V. Cooke

The mosaic piecework tradition came to America from England. This allover
pattern represents the simplest form of the technique. The family history of this
quilt relates that it was started in England but completed in Pennsylvania. Each
tiny hexagon measures 1.75″ and is lined with a paper backing: scraps of letters,
prints, legal forms, newspapers, sheet music, etc. dated 1844, 1846, 1849 and 1850.
The finished quilt traveled with the family from Pennsylvania to Kansas and then
to Massachusetts in 1907.

Courthouse Steps Quilt, pieced log cabin, made by Jennie Sargeant Green, Rutland, Vermont, wool and cotton, c. 1880–1890s (81″ × 81″)
GIFT OF GENEVA TETU

The log-cabin pattern is based on the image of stacked logs. To produce this effect, thin strips of cloth are pieced around a center square. The dark colors in this quilt are predominantly wool fabric in rich jewel colors (shades of blue, violet and green), while the light-colored pieces are cut from white printed cottons. Textile manufacturers often packaged bundles of shirting fabrics to be sold to quilters. This quilt was given to the Museum by the granddaughter of the maker.

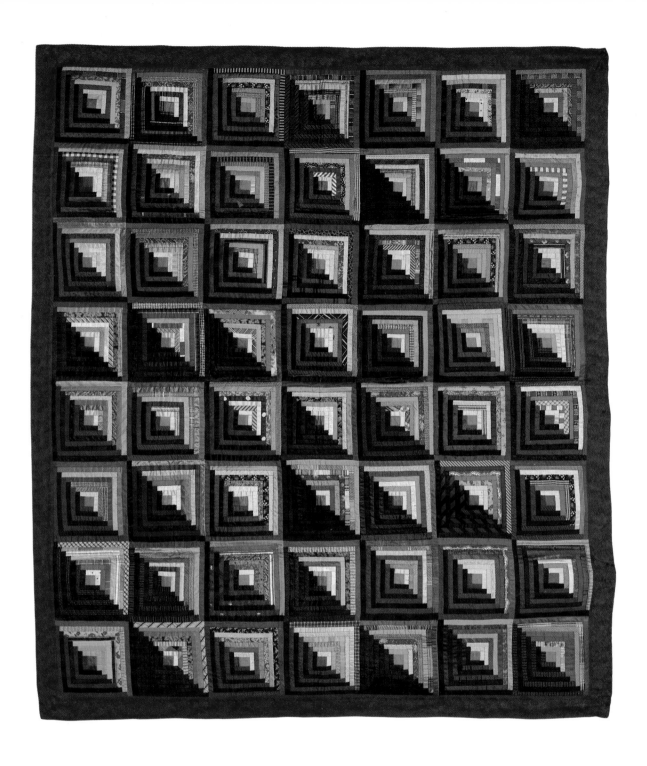

Straight Furrow Quilt, pieced log cabin, made by Jane Furman Allen, West Hempstead, New York, silk, c. 1880–1900 (67½″ × 58½″)
GIFT OF MRS. CARL JOHNSON

Log-cabin patterns were very popular throughout the nineteenth century and typically were made from readily available cotton and wool fabrics. However, the popularity of silk-fabric quilts in the late nineteenth century led many quiltmakers to use luxury fabrics in this familiar pattern. In log-cabin patterns, the completed pattern blocks create a large, dramatic design when sewn together. Fabrics were carefully chosen to emphasize the strong light and dark contrast required to carry out the overall pattern. The names of log-cabin patterns are derived from the appearance of the overall pattern and include Barn Raising, Windmill Blades, Sunshine and Shadow, and Streak o' Lightning.

Haskins Crazy Quilt, pieced, appliqué and embroidered, made by Mrs. Samuel Glover Haskins, Granville, Vermont, cotton and wool, c. 1870–1880s (82" × 69")

During the last third of the nineteenth century, the crazy quilt was by far the most popular type of quilt made in America. Although most crazy-quilt makers relied on brilliantly patterned silk fabrics and elaborately embroidered designs to embellish their creations, Mrs. Samuel Glover Haskins used plain and printed cottons for her quilt blocks and decorated each of the 42 blocks with a different appliquéd motif. Human figures and familiar barnyard animals were interspersed with wild and exotic animals such as moose, mountain lions, camels and giraffes. The maker's choise of fabrics for the appliquéd motifs is creative and amusing: striped cotton for the tiger's body, a wavy-patterned material for human hair and small-patterned calicos to costume the human figures.

Crazy Quilt, pieced and embroidered, made by Mrs. Wadleigh, Tryon, North Carolina, silk, "9 March 1886" (78½" × 55")
GIFT OF GARTH CATE

Designed as ornaments to be draped over a settee or bed, late-nineteenth-century crazy quilts were sewn of individually worked strips or blocks containing a variety of elegant woven fabrics pieced together and decorated in a haphazard fashion. Women did not have to rely on their own supplies of fabric scraps, as American silk manufacturing companies soon began packaging remnants of silk satins, brocades, velvets and other richly decorated woven fabrics for use in quilts. The mid-nineteenth-century presentation album-quilt tradition continued in the latter half of the century. Nine friends presented Mrs. Wadleigh with nine crazy-quilt squares in honor of her tenth wedding anniversary. Mrs. Wadleigh pieced the tenth square, and her husband made her a present of the velvet and satin fabric for the quilt's border and lining.

Crazy Quilt, pieced and embroidered, made by Mrs. Mellon, New Hampshire, silk, c. 1880s (66" × 55")
GIFT OF GEORGE T. MASCOTT

At the 1876 Centennial Exhibition in Philadelphia, the Royal School of Art needlework exhibit displayed superb examples of embroidery and needlework. This inspired the development of decorative arts and needlework societies around the United States, and women quickly began to incorporate these needlework designs into contemporary American quiltmaking traditions, especially crazy quilts. Each seam of this quilt was embroidered with herringbone or feather stitching, and individual fabric pieces were embellished with silk painting, appliqué plush or satin work, ribbon and tinsel embroidery, Kensington shaded embroidery, and outline work. Textile manufacturers, silk-floss companies and ladies' magazines offered elaborate patterns for piecing the quilt and decorating the finished product.

Wild Goose Chase Variation Quilt, pieced and tied, maker unknown, Chatham, New York, silk, c. 1875–1900 (64½″ × 54″)
GIFT OF MRS. WILLIAM BURTON WESTCOTT

Between 1860 and 1900, American textile companies were producing as much silk dress fabric as was being imported. New quilt designs were developed and traditional patterns restyled to take advantage of the lustrous texture and vibrant colors of the silk fabric available. This quilt, a variation of the well known Wild Goose Chase pattern, is pieced of silk necktie fabric, even though the pattern was more often worked in cotton. In 1882, an article in *Harper's Bazar* reported that quilts of the period looked "more like the changing figures of the kaleidoscope, or the beauty and infinite variety of Oriental mosaics."